DANISH
‹DEPENDENCIES›

PLACES AND PEOPLES OF THE WORLD

DANISH DEPENDENCIES

Charlotte Levine

CHELSEA HOUSE PUBLISHERS
New York • Philadelphia

COVER: The town of Vagur is a good example of
the heavy economic expansion that has occurred in recent years
in the Faeroe Islands.

Chelsea House Publishers
Editor-in-Chief: Nancy Toff
Executive Editor: Remmel T. Nunn
Managing Editor: Karyn Gullen Browne
Copy Chief: Juliann Barbato
Picture Editor: Adrian G. Allen
Art Director: Maria Epes
Manufacturing Manager: Gerald Levine

Places and Peoples of the World
Editorial Director: Rebecca Stefoff

Staff For DANISH DEPENDENCIES
Text Editor: Bill Finan
Copy Editor: Nicole Bowen
Deputy Copy Chief: Ellen Scordato
Editorial Assistant: Marie Claire Cebrián
Picture Researcher: Nisa Rauschenberg
Assistant Art Director: Laurie Jewell
Designer: Marie-Hèléne Fredericks
Production Coordinator: Joseph Romano

First Printing

1 3 5 7 9 8 6 4 2

Library of Congress Cataloging-in-Publication Data

Levine, Charlotte R.
Danish dependencies.
Includes index.

Summary: Surveys the history, topography, people, and culture of Danish Dependencies,
with emphasis on their current economy, industry, and place in the political world.

1. Faeroe Islands—Juvenile literature.
2. Greenland—Juvenile literature.
[1. Faeroe Islands. 2. Greenland] I. Title.
DL271.F2L48   1988   949.1'5   87-18289

ISBN 1-55546-787-3

‹CONTENTS›

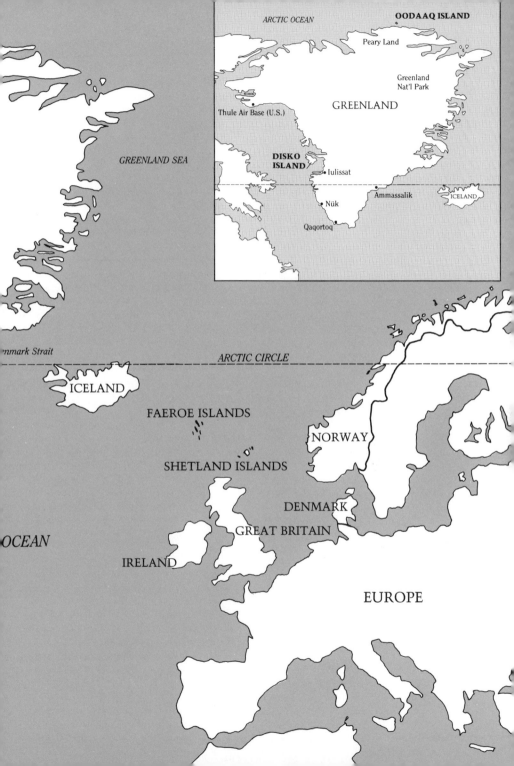

ARCTIC OCEAN

OODAAQ ISLAND

Peary Land

Greenland
Nat'l Park

Thule Air Base (U.S.)

GREENLAND

GREENLAND SEA

DISKO
ISLAND

Iulissat

Ammassalik

ICELAND

Nük

Qaqortoq

Denmark Strait

ARCTIC CIRCLE

ICELAND

FAEROE ISLANDS

SHETLAND ISLANDS

NORWAY

DENMARK

GREAT BRITAIN

OCEAN

IRELAND

EUROPE

◄ FACTS AT A GLANCE ►

Faeroe Islands

Area	540 square miles (1,399 square kilometers)
Population	45,000
Status	Self-governing dependency of the kingdom of Denmark
Capital	Thorshavn
Official Language	Faeroese
Religion	Evangelical Lutheran Church of Denmark, 74.4 percent; Plymouth Brethren, 19.8 percent; Roman Catholic, .01 percent; other, 5.2 percent
Economy	Fish and fish processing, wool and woolen goods, tourism

Greenland

Area	840,000 square miles (2,175,000 square kilometers)
Population	54,000
Status	Self-governing dependency of the kingdom of Denmark
Capital	Nûk
Religion	Lutheran Church of Greenland, 89 percent; animist, 11 percent
Official Language	Greenlandic
Economy	Services, fishing and fish processing

◄HISTORY AT A GLANCE►

4000 B.C. to A.D. 1000	Eskimos migrate from North America and the Canadian arctic to Greenland in successive waves.
early 9th century A.D.	Viking explorer Grim Kamban lands on the Faeroe Islands and founds a colony there.
early 10th century	Viking explorer Gunnbjorn Ulfsson sights Greenland and reports on its existence to Vikings in Iceland.
985	Erik the Red makes landfall in Greenland with 14 Viking ships and founds a colony.
1000	The Faeroese establish their Lagting, or parliament. At about the same time, Leif Eriksson introduces Christianity to the Vikings in Greenland.
1035	Suffering from plague and famine, the Faeroese people unite with Norway.
1261	The Greenland settlers also swear allegiance to Norway. The colonies in Greenland suffer heavy losses due to climate change or disease.
1380	Denmark acquires control of Norway and its territories, including Greenland and the Faeroe Islands.
1410	The last ship known to have visited the Greenland settlements returns to Norway and reports the dire condition of the colonists.
during the 14th century	The Viking colonies in Greenland die out.
1619 to 1708	Denmark leases the Faeroes to a series of Dan-

ish businessmen, who mismanage the islands' economy.

1721   Denmark sends missionary-businessman Hans Egede to Greenland as the first step in recolonizing the island. He converts many of the Eskimos to Christianity.

1814   The Treaty of Kiel confirms Denmark's ownership of the Faeroe Islands and Greenland.

during the 19th century   Explorers of many nations survey Greenland's unknown coasts and interior. The age of polar exploration culminates in Robert Peary's journey to the North Pole in 1909.

1940s   During World War II, the British occupy the Faeroes and Greenland is temporarily protected by the United States.

1948   Denmark grants home rule to the Faeroe Islands.

1979   Denmark grants home rule to Greenland, which elects its first legislature.

DANISH
‹DEPENDENCIES›

This Inuit woman, who carries her baby in the hood of her sealskin parka, lives in Greenland, the world's largest island—and one of Denmark's two North Atlantic dependencies.

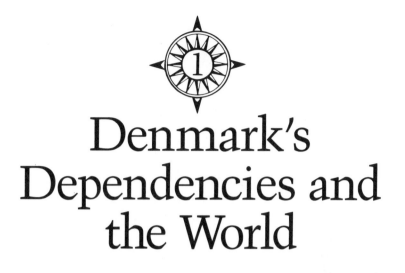

Denmark's Dependencies and the World

Although the Scandinavian nation of Denmark is one of Europe's smaller countries, it possesses two outlying dependencies, or territories, that are part of the kingdom of Denmark. Both of these dependencies are located far from Denmark, in the icy waters of the North Atlantic Ocean. One is a cluster of tiny islands called the Faeroe Islands; the other is the largest island in the world, called Greenland. They are vastly different in size and are 1,500 miles apart, but these 2 dependencies share some elements of common history. Both were settled by Vikings in about the 10th century A.D., and both fell into the hands of the Danes in 1380. In recent years, both the Faeroe Islands and Greenland have been given freedom to govern themselves in local matters, although they remain subject to Denmark in international matters.

Located north and slightly west of the British Isles, about midway between Norway and Iceland, the Faeroe group is made up of 22 islands, with a total land area of 540 square miles (1,399 square kilometers). Because they are washed by the Gulf Stream, the broad current of warm water that flows through the North Atlantic from the tropics, the Faeroe Islands have a climate that is mild, considering their northerly latitude. Summers are cool and winters are damp and stormy. The lush green pastures found in the Faeroes are the result of this wet, mild weather.

The name Faeroe comes from *får*, an ancient Scandinavian word for "sheep." The picturesque island group is inhabited by fishers and farmers of Scandinavian descent whose animals graze on the thick grasses. Sheep farming is the most common and most profitable land-based occupation of the islands; in fact, the national symbol of the Faeroes is the ram, or male sheep. However, fishing is the mainstay of the islands' economy.

The economy of Greenland also depends on fishing. Catching and processing fish for export are major industries. But Greenland is very different from the Faeroe Islands in several important ways. While the Faeroes, like Iceland, are considered to be part of Europe, Greenland is undeniably a part of the New World. It lies north and

Fjords and cliffs give the Faeroe Islands a rugged beauty.

Greenland icebergs are a
hazard to shipping—one
sank the Titanic.

west of the Faeroes and Iceland, off the northeastern coast of the
North American continent. Its total land area is 840,000 square miles
(2,175,600 square kilometers). About four percent of this area consists of small offshore islands, and the rest is a single enormous
landmass.

Much of Greenland lies north of the Arctic Circle. Because of
this, and also because the warming influence of the Gulf Stream
does not reach its shores, Greenland has a climate colder and drier
than that of the Faeroe Islands. Four-fifths of Greenland is covered
with an ice pack that never melts. Along the coast, huge icebergs
break from the pack to float in the surrounding waters. Called "icy
mountains" by the Native American people of Greenland, the icebergs are beautiful, but they are also deadly. As they drift about the
North Atlantic, they can damage or sink ships that use the international shipping routes between Europe and North America. The
iceberg that sank the famous ocean liner *Titanic* in 1912 originated
in the Greenland ice pack.

Greenland is important to the rest of the world as a center of meteorology, or weather research and reporting. Many of the storms that strike Europe gather their strength over Greenland. During World War II, weather stations were established in Greenland to help forecast the weather on the battlefronts of Europe. Today, the information that is broadcast to Europe and the United States from sophisticated meteorological stations in Greenland helps make up many of the world's daily weather reports.

Another internationally important feature of Greenland is its strategic location—that is, its position near the top of the world, along the air route from eastern North America to northern Europe and Russia. During World War II, the United States built an air base at Sondestrom; it was the home base for bombers attacking German targets in Scandinavia. In the summer of 1951, the United States began constructing a series of powerful radar stations that were designed to detect nuclear warheads traveling toward North America. Thule, in the far north of Greenland on the island's west coast, was chosen as the site for one of the stations because it is close to the shortest route between New York City and northern Russia. This station was built with the permission of Denmark and received new, more powerful equipment in the mid-1980s. Today, the radar tower

Radar installations in Greenland monitor the polar skies for missiles.

is 1,250 feet (478 meters) tall, and its range is more than 3,000 miles (4,800 kilometers).

Size and climate are not the only differences between the Faeroe Islands and Greenland. There are profound cultural and ethnic differences as well. Although the populations of the 2 dependencies are similar in size—45,000 for the Faeroe Islands and 54,000 for Greenland—their languages, religions, and ways of life are very different.

The Faeroese people are descended from Scandinavian Vikings, mostly Norwegian, with some Danish ancestry in recent centuries. They live in small old-fashioned towns and rural homesteads, where they continue to work and socialize in centuries-old traditional ways. The people of Greenland are mostly Native Americans, members of the widespread Eskimo ethnic group, but many of them also have some European ancestry. Members of this group—that is, people whose ancestry is mostly Eskimo but also partly European—make up the largest population group of Greenland; they are called Greenlanders. The island also has some resident Europeans, a few Americans, and some groups of pure-blooded Eskimos. Whereas many Greenlanders and Eskimos follow traditional ways of life, others have become increasingly modernized and urbanized. Greenland's cities are larger and more contemporary than the quaint towns of the Faeroes, probably because Denmark has taken a special interest in developing Greenland. Yet television and air travel are beginning to bring the people of the Faeroe Islands closer to the rest of the world, and life in the Faeroes, as in Greenland, undoubtedly will change to some degree as these Danish dependencies interact with other nations and peoples.

The Vikings were Scandinavian raiders and seafarers who brought Greenland and the Faeroe Islands under the control of Norway and then Denmark.

A Common History

Greenland and the Faeroe Islands are distinct lands, each with its unique culture and people. Yet they share a history of Viking colonization and Danish rule. These shared parts of their histories give the two dependencies something in common, in spite of all their differences.

The first known inhabitants of either dependency appeared in Greenland. They were North American Eskimos, natives of the Arctic region, who crossed from the mainland to northwest Greenland. Using Ellesmere Island and the other islands of the Canadian Arctic as stepping-stones, they reached Greenland either by paddling small skin boats during the summer or by walking on the winter ice— probably by both methods. They arrived in a series of migrations, or gradual movements of large populations, that began about 4000 B.C. The first to reach Greenland were nomadic hunters, and they followed the migrating herds of musk-oxen and reindeer all the way to Peary Land, as the northern tip of Greenland is now called; it reaches to within 500 miles (800 kilometers) of the North Pole. Later groups built permanent settlements in the narrow ice-free strip that borders southwestern and southeastern Greenland; they supported themselves by fishing and hunting seals.

Although waves of Eskimo migration continued to reach Greenland until about A.D. 1000, there were several long periods between 4000 B.C. and A.D. 1000 during which migration halted and the population of Greenland sank to very low levels, perhaps because of drastic changes in climate that made the island even colder and icier than usual. One such period of extreme cold and population decline started around A.D. 500 and lasted for about 400 years. By the time this long cold spell ended, the large island was almost completely deserted. But before the Canadian Eskimos got around to recolonizing it, another group of colonists arrived.

The Vikings in Greenland

The Vikings were Scandinavian seafarers of the 8th through the 10th centuries. In addition to raiding and terrorizing the coasts of Europe and the British Isles, they ranged far out to sea in their narrow dragon-prowed boats, seeking new lands and founding colonies. From their colony in Iceland they pushed on into the North Atlantic. In the early 900s, a Viking named Gunnbjørn Ulfsson returned to Iceland and told of seeing a mysterious land covered with ice far to the west.

The legends about Ulfsson's voyage made a deep impression on an Iceland Viking of the next generation. He was called Erik the Red. In 982, after he killed several men in a blood feud, Erik was banished from Iceland for three years. He decided to spend that time searching for the mysterious western land of ice. He succeeded in reaching the southern coast of Greenland and found, in the ice-free coastal strip, rich farmland inhabited only by bears, foxes, caribou, and birds. The waters teemed with fish and seals. Erik spent his three-year exile exploring and decided that this new land was an ideal spot for a Viking colony—with him as its leader.

He returned to Iceland in 985. In one of history's first real estate promotions, he cleverly called his discovery Greenland, to make it

Erik the Red founded a Viking colony in Greenland in 985.

more attractive to potential colonists; ironically, whereas Iceland is very green, Greenland is mostly ice. At any rate, Erik assembled 25 ships full of men, women, and livestock and set sail for Greenland. Although only 14 of the ships survived the voyage, the new colonists were able to start a permanent Viking colony. Erik settled on the western side of the island's southern tip, and a few years later a group of the colonists moved several hundred miles north to establish a second settlement on a large bay on the western coast. Because Greenland has no large trees, the colonists were unable to build new ships or repair their old ones; in addition, there were no towns or cities in North America for them to plunder. So they gave up the Viking life of raiding and trading, built huts of stone and sod, and settled down to cattle breeding and farming.

It was a hard life in a harsh land, but the onetime Vikings endured. After they had been in Greenland for a few years, they began to encounter bands of Eskimos who were slowly migrating south. The two cultures seem to have interacted only rarely and slightly. Although a few battles were fought, there is no evidence of prolonged slaughter by either side. And although some intermarriage took place, for the most part the Europeans and the Eskimos lived separate lives. The population of Greenland was so small that there was plenty of room for both groups; at its peak, the Viking colony numbered about 3,000 people on fewer than 500 farms, and there were probably no more than the same number of Eskimos on the island at the time.

The Vikings in the Faeroe Islands

The Greenland settlements were not the only Viking outposts in the North Atlantic. Nearly 100 years before Erik the Red landed on Greenland's shores, a Viking explorer named Grim Kamban sailed north from Ireland, searching for new lands to colonize. He landed in the island group that we call the Faeroes and found large stretches of grazing land, a sky filled with game birds, and waters with ample fishing and safe anchorages. He also found a peaceful community of Irish Christian monks, who had inhabited the islands for 150 years. In Viking fashion, Kamban and his followers drove the monks out of the islands and took over.

Like the Vikings who settled in Greenland, the new inhabitants of the Faeroes had to change their way of life. Although their climate is milder than that of Greenland, the Faeroes also have only a few small stunted trees, so building large ships was out of the question.

In the 9th century, Vikings drove Christian monks out of the Faeroes. The Norsemen then turned from war to fishing and herding.

The Faeroese men took up fishing, the women tended gardens, and the children herded sheep.

In the year 1000, the Faeroese established a parliament, or lawmaking body, called the Lagting; its president was called the lagmund. The lagting form of government has endured throughout the centuries and continues to govern Faeroese local affairs today.

Ties with Norway and Denmark

After years of isolation, the Faeroese began to make contact with other nations in the 11th century, when famine and disease struck the islands. In 1035, they united with Norway, hoping to gain financial assistance and supplies of needed goods. In the long run, however, the islanders found that their association with Norway was more beneficial to Norway than to them: The kings of Norway required the Faeroese to sell all of their fish, wool, and other products to Norway at the lowest possible price, yet Norway did not provide the islanders with the benefits they had hoped for. In 1270, the Faeroese tried to dissolve their union with Norway, but Norway refused to let the islands go.

During these years, the Greenland colony was founded and maintained contact with Scandinavia. In about 1000, the Viking Leif

Leif Eriksson, son of Erik the Red, brought Christianity to the flourishing Greenland colony around 1000.

Eriksson introduced Christianity to the colonists in Greenland, and the island received its own bishop in 1126. Until 1261, the settlers maintained their independence as a republic, but in that year they vowed allegiance to the king of Norway, who in turn agreed to provide them with wood, cloth, and other supplies they needed from the outside world. For a time, the colonists took part in a flourishing trade, sending beef, leather, furs, and seal oil to Norway in exchange for wood, metal, and food.

Both Greenland and the Faeroe Islands acquired a new ruler in 1380. As a result of political events in Europe, Denmark took control of Norway and all of its North Atlantic possessions. In the colonies, however, the change from Norwegian to Danish rule was gradual and indirect—so much so that the Faeroese people continued to think of themselves as Norwegians for several hundred years. Denmark treated the Faeroe Islands as poorly as Norway had. Beginning in 1619, Denmark leased the islands to Danish businessmen, who were allowed to control and profit from all the Faeroese trade. Each businessman was permitted to govern his little portion of the Faeroes as he pleased. Under the governorship of a merchant named Christopher Gabel, and later of his son Frederick, the islands sank into a deep economic depression. When Frederick Gabel died in 1708, however, the Faeroese managed to take control of their own economy again, although they remained under Danish overlordship.

The Greenland colony fared worse. In the years just before Norway's territories passed into Danish control, the climate of the western North Atlantic region began another of its long, slow changes. Winters grew longer and colder, summers shorter and cooler. It became difficult for the Greenland Vikings to garden and to raise cattle; ice clogged the trade routes; and the colonists began to suffer from sickness and hunger. Slowly but steadily the number of colonists in Greenland decreased—and so did their contacts with the outside world.

A grave marker, one of the ruins left behind by the Vikings, is decorated with carvings of mythical beasts that were part of their religious beliefs.

The last trading ship known to have visited Greenland returned to Norway in 1410. Its captain reported that the colonists had been reduced to miserable circumstances but were struggling to continue. The rest of the story of the Vikings in Greenland is a mystery. They died out sometime in the 15th century, perhaps from starvation, perhaps from disease. They left behind only the ruins of their stone settlements, their burying grounds, and a few inscriptions carved on rocks, from which archaeologists—scientists who study the remains of past cultures—have been unable to piece together the full account of their disappearance.

Denmark Takes Control in Greenland

During the 16th and 17th centuries, Denmark and Norway tried several times to send expeditions to Greenland, but these attempts failed. The mariners of other European nations, however, "rediscovered" Greenland during the great age of North American exploration.

Sir Martin Frobisher searched Greenland's waters for a sea route to Asia.

Sir Martin Frobisher of England landed on the island's west coast in 1578. Other English and Dutch explorers followed in the early years of the next century; these included Henry Hudson, who mapped part of the west coast in 1610. By the end of the 17th century, most of the coastline had become known through the journeys of whaling and sealing ships.

In 1721, Denmark decided to establish a base in Greenland. A Danish-Norwegian missionary named Hans Egede was sent to an outpost on the west coast. He named it Godthåb; it later became Greenland's capital. The Danish government wanted Egede to search for any surviving descendants of the Vikings and then set up trade relations between them and Denmark; he agreed, not because he was interested in promoting trade, but because he wanted to preach the Lutheran gospel to the survivors. He found only Eskimos, however—the white settlers had been dead for centuries.

Egede converted the Eskimos to Christianity, but he was less successful in his trade mission. The Eskimos had already established a profitable trade with the Netherlands and were not interested in changing their trading partners. The Danes tried to force the Eskimos to trade with them by setting up colonies of deported criminals on Greenland's west coast. The Eskimos became infuriated and rebelled, nearly killing Egede. After this incident, the Danes abandoned their trade campaign for a few years. In 1774, however, they succeeded in imposing a trade monopoly on Greenland. This meant that all commerce with the people of the island had to be carried out by Denmark or with its permission. This trade monopoly lasted for almost two centuries. Although it prevented the people of Greenland from having much contact with the rest of the world, it also prevented them from being exploited by commercial trade and caused all their resources to be reserved for their own use.

Like most of the other nations in Europe, Denmark became embroiled in the intermittent wars between England and France in the late 18th and early 19th centuries. The Danes allied themselves with France. The choice proved unfortunate when France was defeated decisively by England. As an ally of the losing side, Denmark suffered serious losses in the aftermath of the Napoleonic Wars. In 1814, the Treaty of Kiel took Norway away from Denmark. The Danes

The Danish parliament debated the future of Norway's former territories.

were, however, allowed to keep the Faeroe Islands and Greenland.

After losing Norway, Denmark experienced a severe economic depression and was unable to devote any resources to developing the Faeroes. But Greenland attracted considerable Danish interest when substantial deposits of cryolite—a mineral that is the primary ingredient of aluminum—were discovered there. The Ivigtut cryolite mine, the island's first industry, was opened under government control in 1864. Also managed by the government were the Eskimos' fishing and sealing industries.

A New Age of Exploration

Danish settlement and influence in Greenland centered on the west coast. This region was warmer and more sheltered than the wild east coast, which was exposed to the gales of the icy North Atlantic. Eskimo settlements, too, were concentrated in the west. Yet there were rumors of Eskimo settlements on the east coast of the island, even of tribes of cannibals living in isolation there. The 19th and early 20th centuries were the era of exploration of the Canadian Arctic and the search for the fabled Northwest Passage—the hoped-for sea route from the North Atlantic to the North Pacific. During these years of exploration and discovery, the Danes and others explored the mysteries of Greenland's unknown coasts and interior.

English and American explorers led the way in the discovery of the geography and the Eskimo peoples of the northwest. At the same time, American (1822), German (1870), and French (1905) expeditions surveyed parts of the east coast. Denmark took a leading part in the exploration of the remote north and south stretches of the east coast; one Danish explorer was Gustav Holm, who in 1884 went to the southeast to investigate the rumors of cannibal Eskimos. He found a group of 416 wretched, starving Eskimos who had resorted to cannibalism out of desperation. Their main food source, the seal, had become almost extinct in their area. Holm taught them fishing

Norwegian Fridtjof Nansen crossed Greenland for the first time, on skis, in 1888.

skills, giving them a new food source and the basis for profitable trade with Denmark.

At the same time, exploration was under way of the great empty ice cap that covers the interior of the island. In 1888, the Norwegian explorer Fridtjof Nansen and five companions, using skis, made the first complete crossing of the island from east to west. In 1892, the American naval officer Robert Peary made a 1,200-mile (1,920-kilometer) crossing at the wide northern part of the island. He traveled by dogsled, with Eskimo guides, and mapped the extent of the ice cap in the north.

His 1892 trip was Peary's first major Greenland expedition. He attempted another crossing in 1893 but was driven back by sickness and storms. In 1895, he set off once again, only to be forced to turn back when most of his dogs died. The trip was not a total loss, however. Peary solved one of Greenland's oldest mysteries. When white men arrived on the island, they discovered that the Eskimos

Robert Peary explored Greenland for almost two decades.

possessed iron tools. Yet they had no mines and no sources of trade. Where did the iron come from? Peary learned of some large stones in the Cape York region that were believed by the Eskimos to be sacred. He found that they were meteorites—giant chunks of rock and metal that had fallen from space in bygone ages. For centuries the Eskimos had "mined" the meteorites for iron. Peary managed to have several of the meteorites, including one that weighed 34 tons, removed to the American Museum of Natural History in New York City.

By this time, Peary was regarded as one of the foremost explorers of northern Greenland and the Arctic region. He also was obsessed by the desire to be the first man to reach the North Pole. Between 1898 and 1902, he tried twice to reach the Pole from Ellesmere Island, just west of Greenland, and failed both times. He did, however, map and explore the region of northern Greenland (now called Peary Land) that includes Oodaaq Island, the northernmost point of land in the world. In 1906 he tried again for the Pole, failed again, and returned to Ellesmere Island by way of Peary Land. Finally, in 1908–09, he made his final attempt to reach the Pole. After a long, hard journey, he made a desperate last-minute dash with almost no supplies and only two Eskimo companions, then returned to announce to the world that he had reached the North Pole on April 6, 1909. One of the last great prizes of exploration had been seized. Peary retired from exploration and died in 1920.

Peary's discovery of the Pole has always been a little mysterious. His notes and navigational sightings, so essential to determining his correct route and position, are surprisingly incomplete and inaccurate. In addition, a rival explorer, Dr. Frederick Cook, claimed to have reached the Pole in 1908, and the accusations and counterclaims of the two men clouded the issue for several years. Before Peary's death, however, the scientific community disproved Cook's claim, and Peary was generally accepted as the rightful discoverer of the Pole. Yet in recent years, researchers who have examined his notebooks have suggested that he might have been mistaken—that he might, in fact, have missed the Pole by as much as 30 to 60 miles (48 to 96 kilometers). Once again a cloud hangs over Peary's claim, but in the absence of definite proof for either possibility, many people still accept him as the discoverer of the North Pole.

Peary's claim to the Pole was disputed by rival explorer Frederick Cook.

Matthew Henson, Peary's partner, was one of the foremost Arctic explorers.

Regardless of the questions that have been raised about his dash to the Pole, Peary is unquestionably one of the great polar explorers of all time. He and his partner in polar exploration, a black American named Matthew Henson, contributed immensely to the world's knowledge of the Canadian Arctic and of northern Greenland in particular. Their many years in Greenland produced valuable photographs, maps, and accounts of the people and their way of life.

The Modern Era

Compared to Greenland, the Faeroe Islands were of little interest to either Denmark or the world in general during the 19th and early 20th centuries. Left pretty much to themselves, the Faeroese continued to regulate their local affairs through their parliament, the Lagting. With a small population and a good marine environment, they developed a stable economy based on fishing. Once they achieved economic independence from Denmark, the Faeroese began thinking about political independence as well. On several occasions, island leaders asked the Danish government if they could fly the Faeroese flag and use the Faeroese language, rather than Danish, in the schools. Denmark refused these requests.

During World War II, the German army occupied Denmark. To keep the Germans from establishing a base in the Faeroes—from which they could harass Allied ships in the North Atlantic—the British took over the islands. In order to distinguish Faeroese vessels from Danish ones, the British allowed the islanders to fly their own flag; at last the Faeroese had achieved a symbol of independence. The war years, when the islands were free of Denmark's supervision, encouraged independent thinking. Although some Faeroese wished to continue under Danish rule, others called for complete independence, and a third group suggested partial independence, or freedom for the islanders to run their own local government while remaining part of Denmark.

After the war, the Faeroese refused to fly the flag of Denmark. When the Danish insisted, the Lagting voted to dissolve the islands' union with Denmark. This vote changed Faeroese history. Although Denmark did not give up its ownership of the islands, it began to take the Faeroese desire for independence more seriously. In 1948, the Faeroe Islands were granted home rule, which gave the islanders the freedom to govern island affairs through the Lagting with little interference from Denmark.

The 20th century brought changes to Greenland also. Denmark's long-standing claim to its trading stations was extended formally to include the entire island by international agreement in 1921. When some Norwegian hunters set up a colony on the east coast in 1931, the International Court of Justice ruled that Norway had violated Denmark's territorial claims, and the Norwegians withdrew. Since that time, no other nation has disputed Denmark's ownership of the huge island.

The great age of exploration drew to a close after the first successful crossings of the island by airplane were made in 1931. Since then, most of the remaining mapping and scientific surveying have been done from the air. The first weather research stations were established in the 1930s, and they became of crucial importance during World War II. A few Germans landed in Denmark in 1940 and set up bases for monitoring weather and relaying radio reports of Allied ship movements. These bases were seized by U.S. forces in 1941, and several German agents who had been operating out of Greenland were imprisoned in the United States. For the rest of the war, while Germany occupied Denmark, the Danes turned Greenland over to the temporary protection of the United States. Although Greenland was returned to Danish sovereignty after the war, the United States retained permission to operate military bases there; today, Denmark and the United States cooperate within the North Atlantic Treaty Organization (NATO) in the military defense of the island.

In 1951, Denmark's long economic monopoly over Greenland's

The United States built this weather and defense station in 1953.

trade ended when the Royal Greenland Trading Company was abolished. The Greenlanders were free to form trade relations with other countries, although Denmark has remained the principal trading partner. In 1953, Greenland's status within the Danish realm was changed. Instead of being a colony, it became an equal part of the kingdom of Denmark. By the 1970s, however, many Greenlanders had come to resent Denmark's control. In the west, where Danish influence has long been strongest, many Greenlanders were angry and worried about the disappearance of the traditional culture in favor of a westernized, Europeanized culture and way of life. Young people held demonstrations demanding more local control of the government. In 1978, Denmark responded to these concerns and gave home rule to Greenland. As in the Faeroe Islands, this meant that Greenland would remain part of the Kingdom of Denmark but would govern itself in all but international and defense matters. The Greenlanders elected their own legislature in April of 1979, and place names of Eskimo origin came into official use. Greenland was renamed Kalâtdlit-Nunât; the capital city, Godthåb, became Nûk.

Today, centuries after they were first colonized by Eskimos and Vikings, Greenland and the Faeroe Islands have satisfactory economies. Each has achieved a certain measure of self-government and enjoys a beneficial relationship with Denmark. Furthermore, each is committed to preserving the best of its unique culture and way of life. Both Greenland and the Faeroe Islands have found a comfortable balance between independence and dependency.

Jagged rocks and the crashing surf below do not deter a hunter from going after sea birds on a volcanic cliff in the Faeroe Islands.

Land and People of the Faeroes

The 22 mountainous, treeless Faeroe Islands are located in the North Atlantic Ocean. They are approximately 372 miles (600 kilometers) west of Norway and 250 miles (430 kilometers) east of Iceland. The closest landmass is the Shetland Islands, 200 miles (320 kilometers) to the southeast.

Geologists believe that the Faeroe Islands were once part of a single large volcanic island. About 65 million years ago, a series of volcanic eruptions caused much of the island to sink. The parts that remained above water are the present-day Faeroes. During the several ice ages that followed, glaciers gouged deep furrows into the rocky islands. When the ice receded and the level of the sea rose, these furrows were partly submerged in the ocean. They form narrow, winding inlets from the sea, with steep rock walls and countless little promontories and bays. These rugged water valleys are called fjords; they contribute greatly to the dramatic scenic beauty of Norway and Greenland as well as to that of the Faeroes.

The highest points in the Faeroes are located in the northwestern islands. Slaettaratindur, the highest peak, is 2,894 feet (882 meters) tall. Most settlements are found on the lower and less rugged

The Vestmanna Mountains on Strømø are a harsh setting for a lonely farmstead.

southwestern shores. Even here, however, the steep, rocky cliffs rise to 500 feet (150 meters) or more. The difficult terrain makes it impossible for the Faeroese to grow enough food to feed the islands' population; only about four percent of the land is flat enough to raise crops. Hunting and fishing are the main sources of food, and sheep—used for their wool and their meat—can be grazed on rolling hills that are too steep for farming. But food is often scarce and must be imported.

Although the Faeroes are close to the Arctic Circle, their climate is tempered by the Gulf Stream and the warm winds that accompany it. Rainfall is plentiful, with an average of 60 inches (152 centimeters) each year. Streams flow through the pastures and cascade over the cliffs into the sea in sparkling waterfalls. Strong winds and fog are common.

The population of 45,000 is spread across 17 of the islands; the other islands—several of which are merely barren rocks—are uninhabited. The largest island is Strømø; it is 30 miles (48 kilometers) across and 7 miles (11 kilometers) wide. Østerø, Sandø, Suderø,

Vågø, and Bordø are among the larger islands. Skuvø, one of the smallest islands, has only a tiny coastal village. The small island of Kunø is noted for a chain of mountains that almost encircles it.

The Faeroese live on farms scattered across the islands or in villages and towns on the coasts. The smallest villages have about 100 inhabitants. Most of them are clusters of small old houses carefully preserved because wood is highly prized, painted with bright colors somewhat faded by the harsh weather, and often, especially in the farmsteads, roofed with sod for insulation. Their residents are fishers, wool workers, farmers, and shopkeepers.

The largest city is Thorshavn, on Strømø, with a population of 15,000. It is the islands' capital and also their financial and cultural center. Thorshavn was founded in A.D. 825. Its name comes from Thor, the Norse god of thunder, weather, and crops, and *havn*, which means "harbor." Thorshavn is located on one of the busiest harbors in the Faeroes. A multitude of boats and ferries passes through the harbor daily, carrying imports, exports, Faeroese on business or errands, and tourists. In the city, solid modern buildings of stone stand

Thorshavn, founded in 825, is the Faeroes' capital and largest city.

side by side with quaint sod-roofed gabled houses of wood.

Thorshavn abounds in historic sites. A monument marks the spot of the first Lagting, which was held in 825. A fort called Skansin was built in 1580 as protection against raiders; it was considered the strongest fort in northern Europe until the 1800s. An old sloop, the *Westward Ho*, has been preserved as a floating museum of the islands' seafaring history.

Located on the southwest corner of Strømø is the village of Kirkjubour, which was the cultural center of the Faeroe Islands before Thorshavn was well established. Kirkjubour has several noteworthy sites. One is an old church that dates from 1275. Nearby is an even older relic—the ruins of a small, square cathedral built of island stone, with high arched windows like those of the great cathedrals of Europe. It was built in 1175. At Vestmanna on the west coast of the island is a more modern site: three large hydroelectric power plants that supply the islands with electricity. North of Vestmanna is an area of high cliffs where hunters stalk wildfowl.

The second-largest island is Østerø, known for its industry and

This village of 400 people is only a few minutes from the capital—by boat. It is on the island of Nolsø.

Stone fences offer the sheep some shelter from wind and rain.

its impressive natural beauty. Slaettaratindur, the highest peak, is on Østerø, and the island also has the two deepest fjords of the Faeroes, Skalafjordur and Funningsfjordur. Fish-processing and wool-working plants are located on Østerø.

The town of Vidareidi on Vidø Island is surrounded by high mountain cliffs. Thus, although the town itself is quiet and placid, its neighbors are huge, noisy colonies of seabirds that nest in the cliffs. Also on Vidø is Enniberg, believed to be the highest cape in the world; it rises 2,460 feet (750 meters) sheer from the sea.

Sandø is the flattest of the Faeroe Islands, with an average height of less than 1,570 feet (480 meters). It is known for the beautiful, calm beaches at the villages of Sandur and Husavik. These villages are rich in historic sites that date from the Viking era, such as a Viking church in Sandur that was built around 1000 and the ruins of an ancient manor house in Husavik. Tourists often come to these villages looking for old Viking artifacts. Residents still live in several small houses that are about 400 years old.

Villages exist on even the smallest of the habitable islands. They are close-knit communities whose inhabitants rely on each other for survival. Unlike the people of Thorshavn, where 20th-century technology has begun to replace Faeroese tradition, the people of the small islands cling to the remnants of a simpler age in their secluded villages.

Sun-dried fish appears often in island meals.

The mainstays of life for the Faeroese are what they have always been: fishing, grazing sheep, and hunting. Denmark provides the islands with economic aid, but the Faeroese are a proud people who prefer to maintain as much independence as possible, even at the cost of giving up an easier and more luxurious way of life. Hard work and providing food for the community are parts of their heritage.

In the more isolated communities, obtaining food is a constant challenge. Root crops, such as potatoes, are the main agricultural products, although hay is grown to feed the livestock. Most Faeroese hunt wildfowl. Guillemots, fulmars, and gannets are hunted, but puffins are the most prized game bird. Named for its puffed-up appearance, this black-headed, white-bodied seabird with a large, brightly colored beak is known for its tender meat. The Faeroese serve it roasted in the skin. Guns and ammunition are expensive and rare. Most hunters use the traditional *fleyq*, a net attached to a long pole. When a hunter catches a bird, he kills it by wringing its neck and then tucks it under his belt to leave his hands free for the next catch.

Hunting is important, but Faeroese life revolves around the sea. The principal catches are cod, herring, and halibut. Older, established fishermen own their own large fishing boats, and younger men hire out to work on them.

The sea holds not only schools of small fish but also whales, which are prized as a delicacy by the Faeroese. Although most nations of the world honor the current ban on commercial whaling, communities such as the Faeroes and the villages of Greenland are permitted by law to hunt and kill whales for local use, using traditional hunting methods. When a school of whales is sighted near the Faeroe Islands, boats set out in pursuit; the captain of the boat that first spotted the whales is in charge of the hunt. The boats force the school into shallow water and then the captain harpoons one of the whales. The hunt is usually over in 15 minutes or less, but eager fishermen have been killed when the wounded prey turned on them.

News of the kill is broadcast to the surrounding communities by telephone or beacon lights. Everyone stops working—children are let out of school, and even the Lagting suspends its parliamentary deliberations for the day. The Faeroese know that the capture of a whale means the beginning of a long day and night of food and festivities, because the fishermen traditionally share the meat with the community and celebrate the successful hunt with an all-night party.

Wildfowl are an important food source. This hunter uses a harness to reach their nests.

Life-style and Arts

The Faeroese language is an example of the islanders' independent spirit. Faeroese is a form of a medieval Norwegian dialect, related to Icelandic and very much like the language that was spoken by the first Vikings to land on the islands. It is the official language of school and government and is always spoken in the homes. The children study Danish in school as their first foreign language, and all adults are expected to be able to speak it.

As a result of their Scandinavian ancestry and their not having mingled to any great extent with other peoples, the Faeroese are generally Scandinavian in appearance: Most of them have fair skin, blond hair, and gray or blue eyes. Typical dress is casual and similar to American styles. Because the people are mainly fishermen and farmers who work in a damp, chilly climate, they usually wear knitted woolen sweaters. Heavy woolen pants or jeans are worn with knee-high rubber boots, and waist-length insulated parkas are worn in the winter.

Until recently, the Faeroese lived in two-room homes built of stones and sod, perhaps with a wooden gable or front wall. The main room was called the *rogstue*, meaning "room with a hole in the roof." Here the family cooked, ate, and slept. The rogstue was windowless and simple, with a few benches for sitting and alcoves or ledges built into the walls for sleeping; household items, however, were often gaily painted or carved. A more fashionably furnished second room had windows and was used only for special occasions and guests. Newer homes are more modern and have more conveniences, but they are still simple and modest.

Old Faeroese customs are still practiced in some of the remotest parts of the islands. For example, it is customary for girls to read their future by studying herbs, eggs, flowers, and birds for omens, or signs, about whom they will marry. When a man is courting a

An old-fashioned island home has stone walls and a sod roof.

woman, he must prove himself by a feat of strength—such as run-
ning a long distance, rowing a boat in treacherous waters, or jump-
ing great heights—before declaring his love for her.

If the man successfully completes this test, he must enter the
woman's home with witnesses. If she invites him to take a comfortable seat, she is interested in marrying him. If, on the other hand,
she directs him to a three-legged stool, she is not interested. In the
past, a woman and her friends would burn the stool after a rejected
suitor left.

Wedding ceremonies are performed by a minister in church.
Traditionally, the bride wore a dress of a dark color with a white
collar and a single pin or brooch; the groom wore a coat with silver
buttons. Today, Faeroese brides favor white silk gowns with lace
veils, like those of many brides in the United States and Europe, and
most grooms wear suits or tuxedos. Immediately after the wedding
ceremony, the bride and groom are surrounded by well-wishers who
fire guns into the air. Before guns were available, it was customary
to beat an inflated sheep's-bladder; the noise was believed to ward
off evil spirits. Today, the gunshots are considered a salute to the
newlyweds. Afterward, the couple stroll about town with a glass and
a bottle of alcohol so that everyone can toast their marriage.

The real wedding festivities start at noon the following day. A meal of many courses, lasting more than seven hours, is followed by a dance that lasts all night. A traditional medieval dance and chant are performed at some time during these festivities; they tell the history and myths of the Vikings, Danes, and other Scandinavians. Although there is drinking of alcohol, the Faeroese rarely drink to the point of intoxication.

Christenings are also important events. If a child is born in an isolated part of the Faeroes, his or her parents may have to wait several months until the traveling *prestur*, or minister, comes to that part of the island. During this waiting period, the child's name is kept secret. If the church is nearby, the child is carried to its christening by the strongest available man; this custom is believed to make the child strong.

Throughout the islands, dramatic performances, choirs, orchestras, and exhibitions are common forms of cultural entertainment. In some villages, there are nearly as many performers as there are audience members. The common theme of most artistic activity is the glorification of Faeroese culture and history.

Two Faeroese writers who have achieved international recognition are Jorgen-Frantz Jacobsen and William Heinesen. Jacobsen wrote of island life in his historical novel *Barbara*. Before his death in 1938, he traveled about the world lecturing and participating in writer's conferences. Heinesen is a contemporary painter and musician who is also known as a writer. His novels, poems, and stories have been translated into several languages.

There are many amateur acting groups in the Faeroes—in fact, there is nearly one drama group for each town. Local actors perform for their fellow townspeople in firehouses, churches, and town halls; the dependency's only real theater is in Thorshavn. Several movie theaters in towns and larger villages show foreign films.

Music is the most common form of artistic expression in the

islands. Choirs and orchestras perform throughout the year, and summer festivals in Thorshavn feature internationally famous folk, blues, and jazz artists. On national holidays, singers performing traditional ballads fill the town squares. The chief summer holiday is Olavsoka Day on July 29. On this day, the Faeroese gather in the crowded streets to sing patriotic, modern, and traditional songs. Dancing is part of most musical events in the Faeroes. This is certainly true of the Olavsoka Day Festival. The Faeroese chain dance, which dates from medieval times and tells the history of the Faeroese people, is performed many times on this day.

Art exhibitions are usually held in the Faeroes' new museum, the Nordic House in Thorshavn. Well-known Faeroese painter S. Joensen Mikines has shown his work there often. He is admired, like Jacobsen the novelist, for his vivid portrayal of life on these lonely North Atlantic islands.

The village of Kirkbujour, on Strømø, was the cultural and religious center of the islands during the Middle Ages. These buildings show traces of 12th-century foundation and architecture.

Faeroese Government and Economy

Although they are a dependency of Denmark, the Faeroe Islands control all local affairs through their elected legislature. They have their own flag—a red cross, bordered with blue, on a white background—and they issue their own money and postage stamps, although Danish currency and stamps are also acceptable. The local government taxes the Faeroese, but about 30 percent of its budget is supplied by grants from Denmark. The Faeroese people are citizens of Denmark, and Denmark administers the islands' police and courts. The Danish government controls interpretation of the constitution, foreign affairs, defense, and national finance.

Within the Danish government is a body called the Office of Nordic Affairs. The high commissioner of this office, who is appointed by the Danish cabinet, is the link between Denmark and the Faeroes' local government; he or she is in charge of administering all Danish government programs in the islands. The Faeroese, in turn, have a voice in national policies; they elect two representatives to the Danish Folketing, or parliament.

The 32 members of the Lagting, the Faeroese parliament, are elected every 4 years. Six political parties are usually represented in

The Faeroese hope that the islands' scenic grandeur will attract tourists.

elections. The most important are the Unionist, which is closely tied to Denmark; the Social Democratic, also aligned with Denmark; the People's, which urges a step-by-step program to achieve complete independence; and the Republican, which also favors complete independence.

The Lagting appoints a president, who is called the lagmund, and other high-ranking officials to handle day-to-day administrative duties. The lagmund belongs to one of the four major parties, and three important administrative posts are assigned to members of the other three major parties. One is responsible for education, social services, and energy; one for agriculture, health, transportation, law, housing, and regional development; and one for finance and culture. In this way, all the major political opinions and groups are represented in the government.

The local government is responsible for the educational system. Faeroese schools include elementary and high schools and a special folk high school for students who want to study music, art, and dance. Training courses are available for nurses, teachers, seamen, and technicians. There is an engineering college and an academy that offers courses in science, philosophy, and religion. Some islanders complete their education in the universities or colleges of Denmark.

The Faeroes' economy has traditionally been based on hunting, fishing, and grazing sheep. Until the 1960s, industry was nonexistent and the standard of living was far below that of other European countries. In the 1960s, however, the government began to build plants for cleaning, packing, and freezing fish. Today, 20 filleting factories are scattered through the islands, and there are two factories for making fish meal and fish oil. These employ many Faeroese and have become the backbone of the economy. Other local industrial products include fishing equipment and ropes and sails for ships. The overall standard of living is now comparable to that of most Europeans.

But the Faeroes face financial challenges. The local government borrowed heavily from Denmark to finance a new communications system, including roads, harbors, tunnels, telephones, and ferries. In 1980, it was estimated that the islands owed 1 billion kroner (the Faeroese currency) to other nations. This debt—roughly 140 million U.S. dollars—is very large for such a small country, but the Faeroe Islands probably will be able to repay it in time if its economy does not suffer a depression.

Fishing, the most important economic activity, accounts for 90 percent of the islands' total exports. The local government has helped the fishermen invest in a large, modern fishing fleet. There are nearly 300 vessels of more than 20 tons each, including line-fishing boats, trawlers, and net-fishing boats. About 1,000 smaller boats make up the rest of the fleet.

The second-largest export is sheep products: bulk wool, wool sweaters, other woolen goods, and some mutton. But most sheep

Shaggy sheep graze outside Thorshavn's Hotel Berg, built for the increasing flow of visitors.

products are used at home; they account for only a small part of the export economy.

Tourism has increased in recent years. Although the islands are not yet widely known, more visitors each year are attracted to their austere beauty, traditional folkways, and hunting and sport-fishing challenges. New hotels are being built, and the government hopes to encourage the growth of a tourist industry.

Trade unions and employment associations ensure fair treatment of Faeroese employees. Associations representing such groups as shipowners and master craftsmen meet with the trade unions to negotiate wage increases and working conditions for fishermen, apprentices, and other workers.

Transportation and Communication

The rocky landscape and the expanses of water that separate the islands have given travel and communication a special character in the Faeroes. There are no superhighways; instead, most roads are winding, narrow dirt tracks traveled by buses, carts, bicycles, and an occasional car. Some roads on the larger islands have recently been

Car ferries make regular trips from island to island.

paved. With the improved standard of living, cars and trucks have become affordable for more islanders. Some Faeroese even own helicopters, and private boats dot the coves, harbors, and waters between the islands.

Despite the increasing number of automobiles, most transportation is public. Buses run between the capital city of Thorshavn and nearly all of the towns and villages on Strømø and Østerø. There are bus routes on most of the smaller islands, too. Often a route includes two or more islands, so that the bus and its passengers must take a large car ferry between islands. Open boats about 30 feet (9 meters) long are also are used to carry residents and tourists from island to island.

There are two airports: Vågø Airport on Vågø Island and Thorshavn Airport on Strømø. Flights to and from Denmark are scheduled every day, and flights to and from Scotland, Iceland, and Norway are scheduled weekly. From May to September, passenger ships make the trip to and from Denmark twice each week.

Daily news broadcasts, music, drama, religious services, and maritime weather reports are broadcast over Faeroese radio. A television network is being built, and an official television station will soon begin broadcasting. In the meantime, private companies broadcasting reruns from Denmark give the Faeroese who own televisions something to watch.

Seven newspapers are published in the Faeroe Islands. Five are published by major political parties and express their various views; two are independent papers. A weekly newspaper is published by the local temperance (antialcohol) society, and two magazines are published locally. Danish and foreign papers and magazines are also available.

Icebergs drift across cloud reflections in an icy bay between two rocky promontories. Greenland's forbidding coastline is deeply indented with such bays and sprinkled with tiny islands.

The Island of Greenland

The world's largest island, Greenland, lies approximately 500 miles (800 kilometers) northwest of the Faeroe Islands and 250 miles (400 kilometers) northeast of Canada. It is bounded on the north by the Arctic Ocean; the North Pole is less than 500 miles (800 kilometers) away. On the east is the Greenland Sea. On the southeast, the wide Denmark Strait separates Greenland from Iceland. On the south is the Atlantic Ocean. On the west, the Davis Strait and Baffin Bay separate Greenland from the North American continent and the islands of the Canadian Arctic. The closest land is Ellesmere Island, only 16 miles (25 kilometers) to the east.

Greenland is 1,660 miles (2,656 kilometers) from north to south at its longest point and 650 miles (1,040 kilometers) from east to west at its widest point. Its easternmost point is almost as far east as Ireland, while its westernmost point is farther west than the city of Boston. Because it is indented by so many fjords, bays, and coves, Greenland possesses a very long coastline. The length of the coastline has been estimated at 24,430 miles (39,088 kilometers), almost exactly the distance around the earth at the equator.

This island dependency is more than 60 times larger than Denmark, its parent country. Very little of Greenland, however, is ac-

At Ilulissat, a new iceberg breaks off the glacier every five minutes.

tually habitable. Of its 840,000 square miles (2,175,600 square kilometers), only about 131,930 square miles (343,018 square kilometers) of the land are free of ice. This ice-free region forms a border around the southern part of the island, about 50 miles (80 kilometers) in width. The rest of the island is permanently covered by a solid mass of ice. The average depth of the Greenland ice cap is about 5,000 feet (1,510 meters). In some parts of the north, however, it is much deeper; the maximum recorded depth is 11,480 feet (3,444 meters). When melted, the ice yields fresh water, not salt. Eskimos melt it and use it for cooking, drinking, and cleaning. Ice from the northern region is also made into ice cap rocks, sometimes called ice cubes. These are large chunks of ice that are chipped out of the cap and shipped to areas of the island where the drinking water is not good.

In many places along the edge of the ice cap, sheets of ice crawl from the center of the island along valleys toward the sea. These slow-moving rivers of ice are called glaciers, and when they reach the sea, chunks break off to form icebergs. One of Greenland's glaciers is believed to be the fastest-moving glacier in the world. It is called the Jakobshavn Glacier, and it has been known to advance as much as 100 feet (33.3 meters) in a single day. Another geographical feature unique to Greenland is the *nunataks*, or high, isolated mountain peaks that emerge from the ice cap in places where the rest of a mountain range is covered. Along the east coast runs a range of mountains that average about 7,000 feet (2,120 meters) high. Mount Gunnbjørn, Greenland's highest point, is part of this range. It is 12,139 feet (3,670 meters) tall. Both the east and west coasts of Greenland are gouged with many long, deep fjords. Their winding waterways, steep cliffs, and drifting icebergs give the coast a magnificent and severe beauty.

Most of Greenland's people and settlements are found along the ice-free southern and western coasts. This region is characterized by deeply cut inlets along a rocky shore. Depending upon the time of year, the landscape is either dull green (summer), brown (spring and fall), or white (winter). Even in the warmest months, only sparse vegetation grows. Willow, alder, and birch scrub—that is, stunted trees usually no taller than people—appear in the south, and mosses and tough grasses grow throughout the ice-free region. Of Greenland's 400 or so plant species, about 300 are native to North America, 50 were brought to the island by the first Viking settlers, and the remaining 50 have survived on isolated nunataks since before the first ice age.

The seas around Greenland are richer in life than the land. Seals and whales were traditionally the main food source for the Eskimos, and in recent years fishing has become very important. The rivers contain salmon and trout, and cod, halibut, flounder, and capelin

Greenland's oldest form of transportation, the dogsled, is still widely used.

are taken from the sea. Only seven land animals are native to Greenland: polar bear, musk-ox, reindeer, arctic fox, snow hare, lemming, and ermine. Among the many species of seabirds that nest in Greenland are auks, gulls, eiders, wild geese, guillemots, and ducks; land birds include snowy owls, ravens, ptarmigans, white-tailed eagles, falcons, snow buntings, and longspurs. The most noteworthy insects are probably the mosquitoes, which during the short summer appear in large numbers.

Greenland's climate is arctic; only in the southwest is it warmed ever so slightly by the effects of the Gulf Stream. January temperatures on the southwest coast average 21°F (−6°C). July readings at the same point average 45°F (7°C). In the far north, January temperatures average −31°F (−35°C), and July temperatures average 39°F (4°C). On the inland ice cap, summers are much colder than on the coast, with average temperatures of 10°F (−12°C) in July; in winter, the average temperature on the ice cap is −53°F (−47°C). Rainfall is light everywhere, ranging from about 10 inches (25 centimeters) a year in the north to about 45 inches (114 centimeters) in the south. Throughout the island, strong winds prevail much of the time, making mild temperatures seem cold and cold temperatures seem bitter. Another feature of Greenlandic weather is frequent, rapid changes. For example, a cloudless blue sky of dazzling sunshine may change within a few minutes to one of heavy, unbroken clouds—and then change back again less than an hour later. This phenomenon is caused by the rapid eastward movement of the low-pressure air masses that originate in the Arctic and are responsible for much of the weather of the northern hemisphere.

The large portion of Greenland that is north of the Arctic Circle experiences continuous darkness from November to February each year. The sun does not rise fully during this time, although the sky lightens briefly for a few weeks in January with reflected light, which is sometimes called the false dawn.

Cities and Towns

Most of Greenland's 54,000 people live in towns on the coast. Although people sometimes enter the interior—Eskimos to hunt and scientists for research purposes—permanent settlements there are impossible because of the ice cap. The only land for building and planting is on the coast. Most of the settlements are small towns or

Many residents of Nûk, the capital, live in Western-style houses with lawns.

villages whose inhabitants are fishers, hunters, or workers in the new fish-processing plants. Most of these towns have their own grocery stores, schools, post offices, health clinics, and banks, so that people do not have to travel often.

In contrast, Greenland's capital is a growing, Western-style urban center. Located on the west coast, it was one of the original Viking settlements. Later, Hans Egede established his headquarters there and named the place Godthåb. It was made Greenland's capital and, when Greenlandic place names replaced Scandinavian ones, it was renamed Nûk. It is picturesquely situated at the entrance to a large fjord, with steep mountains and green valleys on either side.

Nûk is a modern city of industrial factories, government buildings, and urban apartments. Numerous fish-processing plants provide jobs for many of the city's 12,000 inhabitants. The Landsting meets in Nûk in a large white ultramodern building that is part of a complex of government offices. The largest hospital in Greenland, the Queen Ingrid Hospital, is located here, as are several health clinics and dental offices. A teachers' college and an art school also are located in Nûk.

A girl in Qaqortoq wears typical Greenlander clothing: parka and jeans.

The capital is a center of cultural activity and entertainment. Greenland's central museum and library are there; activities and lectures—usually concerned with Greenlandic culture—are held in these institutions. Dance and music performances and exhibits of paintings and sculpture also are frequent in the city. Nûk has four large hotels to accommodate business travelers and Greenland's few tourists.

People in the smaller towns are content to continue a slower, more traditional way of life that emphasizes the Greenlandic cultural heritage, the careful use of natural resources, and an appreciation of the land's stark beauty. Three such towns are Ilulissat, Narsag, and Qaqortoq. Each has its own fish-processing plant, banks, hotels, and shopping centers, yet each is surrounded by parks, natural sites, skiing and hiking trails, and camping grounds. People who want to explore the countryside around these towns can rent dogsleds, boats, or even helicopters.

Ilulissat—the name means "ice mountain" in Greenlandic—is located on the West Coast, north of Nûk; it is famous for a mountain of ice crystals that stands at the edge of town. Ilulissat is also famous as the birthplace of Knud Rasmussen, a famous Arctic explorer of the early 20th century. His home has been turned into a museum. In February, Ilulissat celebrates the return of the sun after the polar night. All the residents climb a hill to watch the sunrise. A great party with singing and dancing follows. Easter and the coming of spring is celebrated with dogsled races. Qaqortoq is located near the southern tip of the island and is noted for the many small museums that house Eskimo artifacts and replicas of Eskimo dwellings. Narsaq, just north of Qaqortoq, is known for the fine fishing offered by many rivers that flow through the town.

The distant ancestors of these Inuit children came from northern Siberia and China by way of Canada. Most Inuit today also have some European ancestry.

Greenland's Inuit People

Greenlandic society is both traditional and modern. Nûk, the capital city, has all the typical features of a modern city: new buildings, cars and buses, cultural events, fine restaurants, broad streets, and museums. It also has some of the less attractive features of modern urban life, including unemployment and housing shortages. The north country, however, is a land of scattered Eskimo settlements. The people here live close to the earth, as their ancestors did for generations, and they depend directly on polar bear, reindeer, seal, and fish for day-to-day survival.

Greenlandic Eskimos, also called Greenlanders, are the island's largest ethnic group. These are the descendants of Eskimos who also have some European ancestry, and they make up more than 75 percent of the total population. There are groups of pure-blooded Eskimos in the far north and in the east, and there is a population of whites, mostly Danes, in Nûk and the larger towns.

All Eskimos, whether Greenlanders or pure blooded, call themselves Inuit. This name means "the folk" or "the real people"; the word *Eskimo* comes from a name once used by other American Indians to refer to the Indians of the far north and is not used by the northerners themselves.

The Inuit are of average height, usually stockily built. They generally have round faces, complexions ranging from yellow to deep brown, dark brown eyes, and straight black hair. Most also have high cheekbones and straight, prominent noses. Like all Native Americans, they are ethnically related to the native peoples of Siberia, Mongolia, and northern China.

As Greenland has moved into the 20th century, the Inuit have struggled to preserve the heritage of their ancient hunting and fishing life. The change of Danish place names to native ones is an example of their recent successes. The official language—the one that is spoken at home, taught in school, and used for government business—is called Greenlandic; it is an Inuit dialect. Many Greenlanders also speak Danish, and a few speak English.

Approximately 90 percent of the population is Christian, largely as a result of the efforts of Danish missionaries in the 19th century. The Church of Greenland, a Protestant church, is part of the Church of Denmark. The native Inuit religion is still observed by many peo-

Every village skyline has a steeple. Most Greenlanders are Protestants.

Snow covers the ground much of the year in this settlement north of Nûk.

ple of northwestern and eastern Greenland. It is a form of *animism*, in which objects and places in the natural world are believed to contain spirits or gods.

The Inuit animists worship many gods, but Tornassuk, or Tupilak, is the chief god. He rules over all guardian spirits, which are called *tornat* and are believed to help humans. But Tornassuk has no power over the sea; that is the domain of the goddess Arnaknagsak. The Inuit pray to her for calm seas and successful fishing and sealing. They believe that each person, animal, and object has *inua*, an inner spiritual or supernatural force. People, the Inuit believe, have two spirits. When a person dies, one spirit stays with the body — or it may enter the body of a newborn child, who then should be named after the dead person. The other spirit lives in a land of the spirits. There are several spirit lands above and below ground.

Each Inuit community has an *angakok*, a shaman or wizard who is believed to be able to communicate with the spirit world. The angakok is usually an older man whose wisdom is respected by all. If evil befalls the community, the angakok is supposed to discover who committed a crime against the gods and spirits and thus brought the bad luck. The guilty person must confess his or her sins to the angakok in public; the angakok then speaks to the gods, urging them to restore peace and prosperity to the community. When an angakok speaks with the spirit world, the Inuit believe, his own soul goes under the earth or to the moon to find the spirits. He talks to them in a special language of very old Inuit words and poetic phrases. An angakok must be trained to use this language by another angakok. Although many Inuit today no longer accept without question all of the old beliefs and practices relating to the spirits, most continue to honor the wisdom and leadership of the angakoks. And most Inuit also cherish the close-knit community bonds that are forged by their traditional beliefs.

The lives of the Inuit revolve around hunting and fishing, particularly on the northwestern and eastern coasts, where there are few towns. Seal hunting and fishing for salmon, cod, shrimp, and shark are the main occupations. In the winter, when much of the coastal sea is frozen, Inuit hunters cut holes in the ice to fish. They also kill seals who come to the holes to breathe. During the summer, they hunt and fish from their *kayaks*. A kayak is a small boat that holds only one or two people. The frame is made of wood or bone, lashed together with heavy string and covered with water-resistant reindeer skins or sealskins. To prevent frostbite in the coldest regions, domes of animal skin are attached to the kayaks, and the hunters peer out from slits in these domes. Only men use kayaks. Women, children, and older people travel in *umiaks*, which are larger boats.

The Inuit also hunt foxes, reindeer, polar bear, rabbits, and birds. At one time they used harpoons and throwing spears made of driftwood, stone, and seal ivory. Bladders filled with air were attached to the weapons, so that, if a hunter accidentally dropped his harpoon in the water, the precious item would float. Today, however, most Inuit hunt with rifles. Pit traps and cages are sometimes used to

(continued on p. 77)

SCENES OF

DANISH DEPENDENCIES

◄ These Inuit children will face the challenge of keeping their traditional culture alive as Greenland's contact with the rest of the world increases.

∨ Qasiqiannguit is one of many small trading stations that allow Greenlanders in the outlying districts to trade their fish and furs for food, fuel, clothing, and other vital supplies. Many coastal towns grew up around trading stations such as this.

▲ *The Danish Youth Hostel service provides cabins for travelers and vacationers in Igaliko, Greenland. The island offers spectacular, unspoiled scenery and outdoor sports such as hiking and cross-country skiing.*

▼ *In Qagssiarssuk, ponies graze on the meadow grasses and wildflowers of Greenland's brief summer.*

⋎ Like a symbol of the traditional Inuit way of life, a lone seal hunter in a kayak must win a living from the cold sea and the ice. Some Inuit have turned their back on homes and jobs in the towns to seek satisfaction in living as their ancestors did.

▲ *The harbor of Suderø, the southernmost of the Faeroe Islands, demonstrates the islanders' dependence on the sea. Boating here is not recreation but part of everyday life.*

▼ *Modern shingled dwellings and old-fashioned sod-roofed stone houses mingle in a Faeroese community.*

▾ *Wildfowl hunting is a traditional and necessary part of Faeroese life. Sea-washed cliffs and lonely mountain meadows are the homes of nesting birds that contribute to the local diet.*

↟ *These puffins have reason to be wary. They nest by the thousands on the sea cliffs of the Faeroes. But they are considered a delicacy and, if they are not alert to the presence of a stalking hunter, they may end up roasted and served for dinner. Farming is difficult in the cold, damp Faeroes, and imported food is expensive, so the islanders make use of every resource that their environment offers.*

Seal hunters in kayaks set out in the gloom of a midwinter morning.

(continued from p. 68)

catch foxes and rabbits, nooses are used to snare birds, and nets are used to fish. The diet of the northern Inuit consists mainly of seal and fish. Seal meat is usually boiled, although the seal's brains and liver may be served frozen. Raw fat, root plants, and algae are also consumed. Melted snow is the common drink. Inuit culture promotes sharing, and a successful hunter or fisherman shares his catch among all residents of the settlement. In southern Greenland, particularly around Qaqortoq, some Inuit have sheep and reindeer farms. Lamb and reindeer meat are produced, mainly for domestic consumption.

The roles of rural Inuit men and women are well defined. The men hunt, and the women care for the children, make the family's clothing, and prepare the meals. Cooking is usually done over open fires. Among Inuit who follow the traditional way of life, one of a woman's most important possessions is her lamp. Lamps are usually carved from soapstone, although some craftsmen use wood, clay, or bone for lamp bases. Seal blubber fuels the fire. An Inuit woman sews, cooks, and cleans by her lamp's light. All married women possess their own lamps, and the phrase "a woman without a lamp" suggests extreme poverty.

<78>

A traditional Inuit family moves the cooking fire outside the tent in summer.

Most people believe that the typical Inuit home is the *igloo*, a low, rounded dome of ice blocks. But only the few Inuit who live on the edges of the ice cap dwell in igloos. Those along the coast used to build their homes from earth, stones, and driftwood or scrub trees. Today, wood and tar paper are used in the south; in the north, where imported lumber is not available and even scrub trees do not grow, stone is still used. Most rural Inuit homes are small, with one or two rooms and few modern conveniences.

In the larger settlements of the western and southwestern coasts, life has a European or American flavor. Men and women work side by side in factories. The small but modern homes have well-tended lawns, and self-service supermarkets sell packaged foods. Urban Inuit dress in blue jeans, brightly colored woolen sweaters, parkas, and boots instead of in the stitched-together skins and furs of their rural counterparts.

This contrast between the old and the new, the traditional and the modern, is a source of some tension and concern for most Inuit. While nearly all of them agree that the benefits of modern health care and education are worthwhile, many fear that the spread of television, snowmobiles, and supermarkets will destroy the traditional Inuit way of life. In parts of the northwest and northeast, these and other modern conveniences are not yet available—and they are not desired by the older Inuit, who fear that the Westernization that is taking place in west Greenland will destroy the land, the sea, and the Inuit philosophy. Some groups of Inuit are trying to ban industries and urban development, at least from parts of the island. They hope to make it possible for young people who wish to live off the land and continue their parents' and grandparents' way of life to do so without contact with the modern world.

Cultural Life

Group games are popular with the Greenlanders. Dice, football, foot-races, arrow tossing, skiing, and soccer are among the favorite pastimes. The Greenland Sports Federation has more than 100 clubs and approximately 20,000 members, most of whom are skiers or soccer players.

The powerful art of the Inuit has thrived for centuries in Greenland's stern environment. Greenlandic art expresses Inuit history and tradition; it shows little or no Scandinavian influence. Sculpture, drawings, and stories tell of both the harshness of life in the Arctic and the joy the Inuit take in natural beauty, communal sharing, and religious experiences.

Music is universally popular among Greenlanders, who enjoy attending and participating in choral and instrumental concerts. Tra-

Inuit women on the east coast have traded sealskins for this accordion.

ditional Inuit music consisted of a chant accompanied by a drum. Today, guitar, piano, and orchestral arrangements are popular, although choral performances attract the largest audiences. Rock music is gaining acceptance in the larger towns. In rural regions, however, the older Inuit keep the tradition of chanting alive. Greenlanders also like to act in or watch plays. The island has no dramatic or movie theaters, but plays and movies are given in town halls and schools. Considering its sparse population and rigorous climate, Greenland is rich in art and culture.

Sculpture plays an important part in Inuit religious tradition. An artist who creates a statue of Tornassuk, the chief god and protective spirit, is considered to be performing a sacred act, and the statue is believed to protect its owner from evil. Animals, scenes of daily life, and other gods and spirits are also typical subjects for sculpture. Lamps, eating utensils, and hunting tools are carved from soapstone or bone or molded from clay. The Inuit believe that everyday objects, not just art objects, should be crafted with beauty and style. Many Inuit implements, tools, and household objects are considered works of fine art by the world's museums.

Sculpture is not only decorative but also part of religious tradition.

Inuit drawings—usually done in black pencil or charcoal, although some artists use colored pencils—tell stories of life in Greenland: a hunter traveling on a dogsled in search of seal, a bear attacking a woman, an angakok praying for good fortune for his people. Artists sell their work in Nûk and the larger towns, and many regional museums scattered about the island contain samples of drawings, carvings, and sculpture.

Storytelling is another important part of Greenlandic culture. Families gather to hear tales of the spirits and the mythical heroes. These stories have been passed down by word of mouth from generation to generation; in this way, customs and rituals have been preserved for centuries. Some of the stories have grim themes—husbands stabbing their wives, women going insane, hunters struggling with wild beasts. These usually contain moral lessons, or warnings against the evils of wife beating, jealously, or violence. Other stories celebrate the joys of a successful seal hunt, of lovemaking, or of the return of spring. Along with stories, the magical lore of chants, charms, and spells is recounted around the fire on long winter nights. The Inuit language was spoken but not written until the mid-19th century, when an Inuit grammar and dictionary were compiled. This gave all the Inuit of the island a shared written language, which is now called Greenlandic. Today, Greenland has a new tradition of written works, many of which preserve the traditional stories on paper. The island has a good public library system, with a central library in Nûk and 17 regional libraries. Books in Greenlandic, Danish, and other languages are available to most Greenlanders.

Greenland's only exports are fish from its bountiful waters and a few minerals from its bleak landscape. Greenlanders depend for economic survival upon aid from Denmark.

Government and Economy in Greenland

Although it is a dependency of Denmark, Greenland enjoys considerable independence and self-government. Since 1979, the island's government has had complete control of almost all domestic affairs; only foreign affairs remain under Danish control. But the political, financial, and social ties between Denmark and Greenland are extensive because of the island's long history as a Danish territory and province.

Greenland's present political system is based on the 1979 Home Rule Act, which gave Greenland the right to control its local government. Home rule gave Greenlanders more control of their own economic resources as well, along with responsibility for social programs such as welfare and housing. Although these programs are administered locally, Denmark continues to be a vital source of financial aid.

The basic principle of home rule is the establishment of mutual respect between Greenland and Denmark, especially in regard to the mineral and oil resources that have been found in Greenland. The Greenlanders want Denmark to recognize that they have the right to profit from these resources, if they are ever exploited.

In 1979, Greenlanders cheered the Home Rule Act by torchlight.

Denmark's dealings with Greenland take place through an office in the Danish government called the Ministry for Greenland. This ministry operates several agencies, including the Royal Greenland Trade Department and the Greenland Fisheries Survey. A high commissioner called a *rigsombudsman* represents the Danish government in Greenland. In return, Greenland sends two representatives to the Danish parliament.

The system of local government closely resembles Denmark's. The legislative assembly, called the Landsting, has 26 representatives who are elected from the island's 8 provinces, or administrative divisions. Four political parties are represented in the Landsting. They are the Forward party, which wants to gain as much independence from Denmark as possible without sacrificing the economic benefits Denmark provides; the Feeling of Community party, which works for closer relations with Denmark and wants Greenland to become part of the European Economic Community, or Common Market; the Wage Earners party, which wants Greenland to stay out of the Common Market; and the Marxist-Leninist Inuit movement, which promotes total independence from Denmark.

The Landsting elects a six-member executive body called the Landsstyre, which is responsible for economic administration, com-

Two Greenlanders attend Denmark's parliament, which meets in this building.

munity relations, and social services. One member of the Landsstyre is the prime minister, who governs the island on a day-by-day basis. The prime minister oversees national and urban planning, relations with the media and with Denmark, matters involving natural resources, and all elections. Each of the other five members of the Landsstyre heads a government office.

The Fisheries, Trade, and Industry office oversees the management of sheep and reindeer, hunting and fishing, and exports. It is in charge of the development and promotion of trade and industry and acts as a consulting service to aid large and small businesses. This office also handles tourism and transportation.

The Economics and Housing office is in charge of wages, working conditions, housing, construction and transportation taxes, economic planning, budgeting, imports, and accounting.

The third office is called Settlements and Outlying Districts, Labor Market, and Youth Affairs. It handles all administrative matters for the small outlying settlements in Greenland's more remote districts, as well as operating employment offices all over the island.

The Social Affairs office administers welfare and social-assistance programs, housing subsidies, industrial injuries insurance, and

About 2,500 people work on commercial fishing craft such as these.

health services. It oversees the operation of the Queen Ingrid Hospital in Nûk, of the smaller hospitals and clinics around the island, and of the district medical officers who travel to outlying settlements by boat. This office also handles administrative matters for Greenlanders living, working, or studying in Denmark.

The fifth office is Cultural Affairs, Church, and Education. It is responsible for cultural grants, communications, films, theater, music, museums, libraries, and the archive that houses Greenland's historic records and artifacts. It controls the board of education and oversees lower and higher education. All students in Greenland are required to attend school for nine years; an additional four-year program is voluntary. The island has two folk high schools for students who want to study traditional arts; it also has training programs for teachers, seamen, clerks, engineers, health-care workers, and builders. Students who want to attend college must do so in Denmark, although there are plans for a university in Nûk.

The judicial system consists of 18 circuit, or district, courts and a high court, which is located in Nûk. Decisions made by the high court may be overturned only by the Danish Supreme Court in Copenhagen. Greenland has an extremely low crime rate. There are no prisons on the island; instead, criminals are confined to correctional houses. During the day, they are employed by the state, and they return to their quarters voluntarily at night. Those who have committed violent crimes are usually sent to Copenhagen to serve their sentence.

Greenland's national defense is controlled by Denmark. But there is a small Greenlandic military department that is concerned largely with inspecting fisheries, rescuing people at sea, and operating weather and communications bases. Greenlandic ships and aircraft monitor the coastal waters, and the Sirius Sled Patrol, a team of men with dogsleds, monitors the most desolate regions of the northeast.

The Danish national radio system broadcasts news, music, religious services, and talk shows in Greenlandic and Danish. The same system provides television broadcasts—chiefly reruns of Danish shows, although some Greenlandic shows are produced. The two major newspapers are a national weekly and a weekly distributed in Nûk. Other local weeklies are published in various areas, and the two major political parties—the Forward party and the Feeling of Community party—publish magazines.

This weather station has been built mostly underground for insulation.

Economy and Transportation

Greenland's cold temperatures, remote location, and permanent ice cap have severely limited its economic growth. There is no large-scale farming because of the cold and because only a small amount of the land can be used. Although mineral resources exist—notably coal, lead, zinc, and possibly oil—mining them is not very profitable because transportation costs are high. Despite these economic limits, Greenlanders manage to have an average annual income equal to 9,200 U.S. dollars, and the standard of living in Nûk and other urban areas is comparable to that of Denmark and most of Europe.

Services such as law and accounting and government jobs employ 33 percent of Greenlandic workers, followed by construction (15 percent), hunting and fishing (15 percent), and manufacturing (14 percent). Trade is an important part of the Greenlandic economy. The island cannot produce enough food to feed its people, so food

Dried fish take the place of fresh ones during times of rough weather.

must be imported. Greenland also imports clothing, housewares, appliances, and machinery. The only exports are fish and fish products and minerals. Almost all of Greenland's trade is carried out with Denmark, but France, West Germany, the United States, and Finland also are trading partners.

With the aid of the Danish government, the fish-processing industry has expanded greatly in recent years. Plants are located on both coasts; 16 of them are privately owned, 4 are cooperatively owned and managed by workers' organizations, and 87 are run by the state. They produce frozen whole fish, frozen fish fillets, salted fish, and frozen shrimp. Most of the frozen cod fillets are sold to the United States; the frozen salmon and shrimp go to Denmark for re-export to other countries. The fishing industry employs about 2,500 commercial fishermen and about 12,000 shipping and processing workers.

Some 800 Greenlanders are employed in the traditional activity of hunting seal and other animals. Annual seal catches total about 90,000 adults. Although seal meat continues to be an important part of the Greenlandic diet, the export market for sealskin has declined in recent years because of the vigorous campaign against the slaughter of baby seals off the Canadian coast. The Greenlanders traditionally kill only adults, preferably males.

Pasturage is limited, but some sheep and reindeer graze in southern Greenland. Sheep raising is difficult in Greenland, where periods of frost followed by sudden thaws can kill most of a herd in a single season. To help farmers protect their flocks from the weather, the government has begun a 10-year program to develop pastures and meadows and to build better sheep shelters. About 20,000 lambs each year provide meat for local use.

Greenland is believed to be rich in minerals, but the cost of mining and shipping them is very high. Cryolite, which was a financial windfall for the island in the 19th century, is no longer regularly mined, although stocks of the mineral are exported from time to time. The only mine now active in Greenland is the Black Angel Mine, named for its entrance, which is shaped like an angel with outspread wings. It employs 320 people and yields 600,000 tons of lead and zinc ore each year. The Black Angel was started in 1973 and is expected to last only a few more years.

Oil drilling has become a sensitive issue in Greenland. Geologists believe that a great deal of oil exists in reserves buried beneath the Davis Strait. In 1976, Denmark funded an attempt to find the oil. After drilling for more than a year, the project's leaders had found no oil, and the project was abandoned. But foreign oil companies think that the oil is there and have been trying hard to buy or lease large tracts of land and offshore rights to continue drilling. Some Greenlanders feel that oil development would bring economic benefits, but others fear that the land will lose its beauty if oil is discovered and large-scale drilling occurs.

Many of Greenland's economic decisions are influenced by Denmark. Greenland can meet only about 10 percent of its financial

The United States maintains a large base at Thule, in the northwest.

needs, and Denmark makes up the difference. A number of Danes live and work in Greenland; many of them are professional and technical workers such as nurses or engineers.

The ice cap makes land transportation difficult. The only roads on the island are found within the cities and towns. To travel between settlements, people must use helicopters, airplanes, ships, snow-mobiles, or dogsleds. In the winter, especially in the north, hunters use dogsleds. Dogsled tours for visitors to the island are available in Ilulissat and other towns.

The island has seven major airports, four in the south, two in the north, and one at Thule Air Base in the northwest. Nûk's airport is the busiest. International flights to Canada, Iceland, and Denmark are scheduled three times weekly in winter and six times weekly in summer. Local flights cover the west coast every day and the east coast twice a week.

Boats and ships are common modes of travel and transportation. The Royal Greenland Trade Department operates two passenger liners on the west coast. Villages on the east coast are connected by local boating services. Many villagers own their own small boats.

The Greenland Technical Organization operates the island's telephone, telex, telegraph, air-rescue alarm, and coastal radio services. All towns and villages have access to telephones and telex systems, and Greenlanders can dial direct to Denmark.

Some of the world's most sophisticated and up-to-date weather stations are located in Greenland. An observation service called the Meteorological Institute is in charge of the four largest stations; other, smaller stations are operated by research groups and universities from many countries.

The Faeroese treasure their traditional way of life—and hope to preserve it.

Past, Present, and Future

The relationship between Denmark and its dependencies has allowed the tiny European nation to extend its influence across the North Atlantic and has given the Faeroe Islands and Greenland many economic benefits. Since the mid-20th century, the two dependencies have received home rule and now enjoy considerable freedom of self-government. This balance between independence and dependency has been shaped by years of conflict, negotiation, and compromise. Although some people in the Faeroe Islands and Greenland would like to see the dependencies cut the ties with Denmark completely, that is unlikely to occur in the foreseeable future. By and large, both Denmark and its dependencies are comfortable with their present relationship.

Denmark gained control over ice-covered Greenland and the rocky, rugged Faeroes after years of fighting in Scandinavia and Europe. At first, the Danes paid little attention to their colonies. Only when cryolite was found in Greenland did Denmark realize that Greenland could be economically important. In recent decades, however, Denmark has tried to improve the economies of the dependencies. Danish aid has improved the standard of living in both, and the prospects for economic stability are good.

The rugged, desolate environments of Greenland and the Faeroes have created some similar attitudes and habits in their inhabitants. Although the Faeroese are of Scandinavian descent and the Greenlanders are of primarily Eskimo descent, both peoples maintain close-knit societies with many small communities, in which customs such as food sharing are still practiced. Both are fiercely loyal to their heritages and are determined to preserve old customs, stories, artifacts, and relics.

But although the preservation of tradition is important to both Faeroese and Greenlanders, both dependencies are experiencing changes. In the Faeroes, a new communications system and increasing tourism will certainly bring about greater exposure to the outside world and its many different ways of life. In Greenland, the presence of Danish professionals and the increase in trade with Denmark and other foreign countries has modernized and urbanized much of the west coast.

Medieval chain dancing survives only in the Faeroe Islands.

Traditional dogsled travel is now a popular tourist attraction in Greenland.

Change is not altogether welcome in the Faeroes and Greenland. Although many people hope that change will mean jobs, education, and a chance at a more comfortable life, others fear that their cultural heritage and traditional values will be sacrificed to modern technology. Only time will tell whether the old and the new will continue to exist side by side in Denmark's North Atlantic dependencies.

◄ G L O S S A R Y ►

angakok   The spiritual guide of a traditional Inuit community, usually an older man. He is trained in the special language of the spirit world.

animism   Religion in which objects, animals, and places are believed to contain gods or spirits that can interact with the human world.

cryolite   A mineral that is the primary ingredient of aluminum.

fàr   A Scandinavian word meaning "sheep," from which the name of the Faeroe Islands is derived.

inua   A spiritual or supernatural force believed by the Inuit animists to pervade all people, animals, and things.

Kalâtdlit-Nunât   The Greenlandic name for Greenland.

kayak   A small boat covered with water-resistant skins and used by hunters in rural Greenland.

Lagting   The Faeroese parliament.

Landsstyre   The Greenlandic parliament.

prestur   A Faeroese word meaning "minister."

rogstue   The all-purpose main room of a traditional Faeroese house.

Tornassuk (also called Tupilak)   The chief god of the traditional Inuit religion.

tornat   Protective or guardian spirits in the traditional Inuit religion.

◄ I N D E X ►

PICTURE CREDITS

Art Resource: p. 27; The Bettmann Archive: pp. 14, 20, 23, 24, 25, 28, 29, 31, 32, 33, 34, 78, 79, 85; The Danish Tourist Board: cover, pp. 2, 16, 17, 38, 40, 42, 43, 44, 50, 52, 53, 54, 58, 60, 61, 62, 64, 67, 69, 70–71, 71 (above, below), 72–73, 74 (above, below), 74–75, 86, 88, 92, 94, 95; Library of Congress: p. 56; Royal Danish Embassy: pp. 41, 45, 47, 66, 77, 80; Donna Sinisgalli: pp. 6–7; UPI/Bettmann Newsphotos: pp. 18, 36, 82, 84, 87, 90